Right at
Home

by Jennifer Waters

Content and Reading Adviser: Mary Beth Fletcher, Ed.D.
Educational Consultant/Reading Specialist
The Carroll School, Lincoln, Massachusetts

COMPASS POINT BOOKS

Minneapolis, Minnesota

Compass Point Books
3722 West 50th Street, #115
Minneapolis, MN 55410

Visit Compass Point Books on the Internet at *www.compasspointbooks.com*
or e-mail your request to *custserv@compasspointbooks.com*

Photographs ©: Keren Su/Corbis, cover; Michael S. Lewis/Corbis, 4; Philip James Corwin/
Corbis, 5; PhotoDisc/Getty Images, 7; Paul Seheult/Corbis, 9; TRIP, 10, 18, 19 (bottom);
TRIP/H. Rogers, 11; Corel, 13; Tim Page/Corbis, 15; Chris Lisle/Corbis, 17;
Roger Ressmeyer/Corbis, 19 (top); Two Coyotes Studio/Mary Foley, 21.

Project Manager: Rebecca Weber McEwen
Editor: Heidi Schoof
Photo Researcher: Image Select International Limited
Photo Selectors: Rebecca Weber McEwen and Heidi Schoof
Designer: Jaime Martens
Illustrator: Anna-Maria Crum

Library of Congress Cataloging-in-Publication Data

Waters, Jennifer.
  Right at home / by Jennifer Waters.
      p. cm. — (Spyglass books)
Summary: Describes various types of houses around the world.
Includes bibliographical references and index.
  ISBN 0-7565-0380-9
1. Dwellings—Juvenile literature. [1. Dwellings.] I. Title.
II. Series.
  GT172 .W38 2002
  392.3'6—dc21
                          2002002556

Contents

House

A house is a **building** where people live. A house can be small or big. There are many kinds of houses.

Apartment

An apartment is a room or group of rooms in a bigger building.

Many families can live in an apartment building. Each family has its own apartment.

Mobile Home

A *mobile* home is a house that is made to be moved easily.

Mobile homes usually stay parked in one spot for a long time.

Houseboat

A houseboat is a boat that is also a house where people can live.

A houseboat spends most of the time near land.

Dome Home

A house can have a round roof. It is called a *dome.*

Many people in snowy or windy places build dome homes. These homes are strong. They are also very warm.

Grass House

Some people live where there are few trees. These people use grass to build their homes.

Grass walls let in cool *breezes.* Grass roofs keep out the rain.

Stilt House

Some houses are built on stilts, or long poles. The stilts keep the house high up in the air.

People who live close to water might live in a stilt house. Stilts keep the water out of the house.

Look at These Homes!

The walls of this small
house are built in a circle.

This house is made of old tires and cans. It is good for Earth, because it is made of things that most people throw away.

This house is made of ice.
In the summer, it *melts* away.

Dream Home

1. Think about your dream home. What kind of home would you like to have? Does it have fun places? Could it float in space?

2. List things you want in your home.

3. Draw your home.

4. Label the things from your list.

Glossary

breeze–a light wind

building–a place with a roof and walls, such as a house

dome–something that is built in the shape of half of a ball

melt–when something solid gets warm and changes into a liquid

mobile–(mo-bill) when something can move or be moved

Learn More

Books

Cordoba, Yasmine A. *Igloo.* Illustrated by Kimberly L. Dawson Kurnizki. Vero Beach, Florida: The Rourke Book Company, 2001.

Jackson, Thomas Campbell. *Hammers, Nails, Planks, and Paint.* Illustrated by Randy Chewning. New York: Scholastic, 1994.

Williams, John. *Houses and Homes.* Austin, Tex.: Raintree Steck-Vaughn, 1998.

Web Sites

kids.discovery.com/KIDS/adv3.html

www.onlineclass.com/doodle/doodle.html

Index

GR: F

Word Count: 194

From Jennifer Waters

I live near the Rocky Mountains,
but the ocean is my favorite place.
I like to write songs and books.
I hope you enjoyed this book.